To Michael and Debra
Robert, Nicole, and Joel
with love

COMETS, METEORS, AND ASTEROIDS

S E Y M O U R   S I M O N

MORROW JUNIOR BOOKS
New York

Photo and Art Credits
Permission to use the following photographs is gratefully acknowledged:
pages 4, 19, 21, 23, and 30, Dennis Milon; pages 7, 8, 11, 15, and 32,
National Optical Astronomy Observatories; pages 24, 25, and 27,
Division of Polar Programs/National Science Foundation; page 26,
NASA; page 29, NASA/Jet Propulsion Laboratory.
Art on pages 12 and 16 by Ann Neumann.

The text type is 18-point Garamond Book.

1 2 3 4 5 6 7 8 9 10

Library of Congress Cataloging-in-Publication Data
Simon, Seymour.
Comets, meteors, and asteroids / Seymour Simon.
p. cm.
ISBN 0-688-12709-6 (trade)—ISBN 0-688-12710-X (library)
1. Comets—Juvenile literature.   2. Meteors—Juvenile literature.
3. Asteroids—Juvenile literature.   [1. Comets.   2. Meteors.   3. Asteroids.]   I. Title.
QB721.5.S54 1994   523.6—dc20   93-51251   CIP AC

Comets, meteors, and asteroids are voyagers from space. Comets are shining patches of light that appear in the night sky from time to time. Most comets are too faint to be seen without a telescope, but some are bright enough to be visible to the unaided eye. This photo of Comet West was taken in March 1976.

Meteors are much more common than comets. They look like thin streaks of light and last only an instant in the night sky. On a clear night you can usually see a few meteors, and on certain nights you can see a dozen or more in an hour.

Asteroids are chunks of rock that circle the Sun. They are sometimes called minor planets, but most are only a few miles across, much smaller than any planet.

Comets have been recorded all through history. Because people rarely saw a comet, many believed that the appearance of a great comet forecast a terrible event such as a war, an earthquake, or a plague.

Aristotle, a Greek philosopher who lived more than two thousand years ago, believed that comets were patches of burning gases in the Earth's atmosphere. Aristotle's ideas about comets were thought to be true for more than eighteen centuries. But in 1577 a Danish astronomer, Tycho Brahe, proved that comets were bodies traveling in outer space, farther from Earth than the Moon.

In 1682 another great comet appeared. Edmond Halley, an English astronomer, studied its path and the reports of comets that had appeared in 1456, 1531, and 1607. He concluded that these were reappearances of the same comet as it orbited the Sun, and he predicted its return in 1758. The comet did come back that year, and it was named Halley in his honor.

Halley's comet in early January 1986.

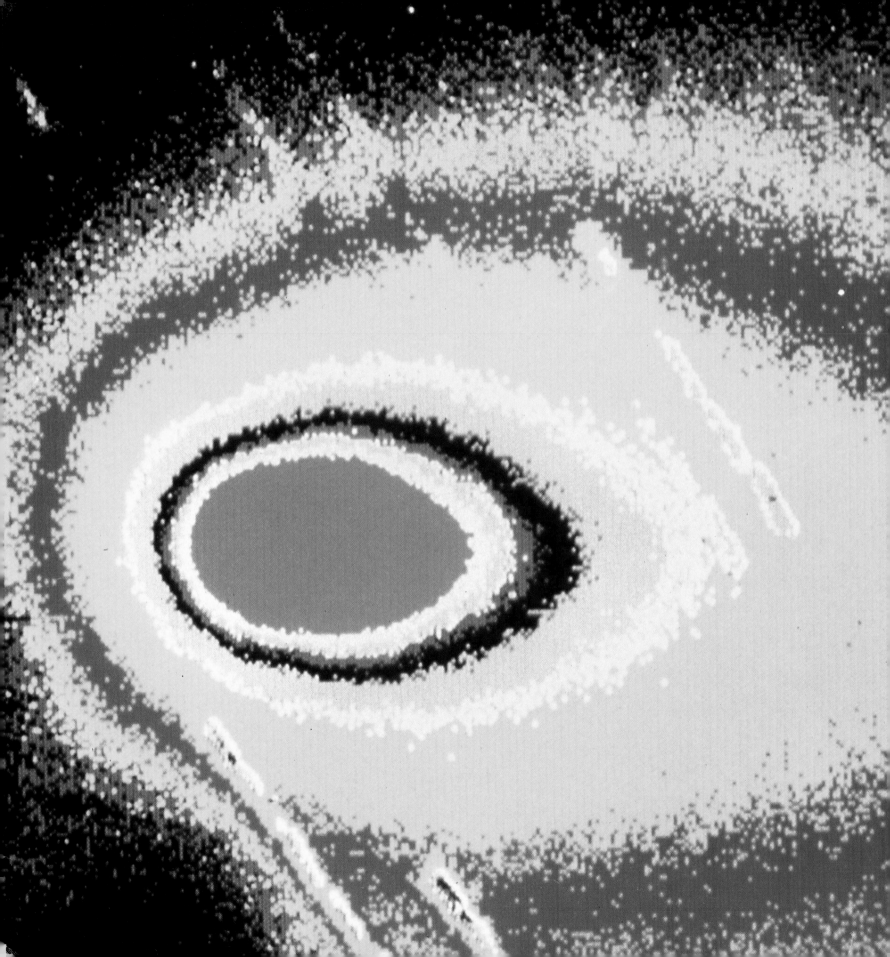

There are hundreds of comets, but we cannot usually see them. That's because a comet in the outer regions of the Solar System is only a few miles wide and too small to be seen from distant Earth. Far out in space, a comet looks like a large, dirty snowball. It has an icy core, or nucleus, covered by a layer of black dust. The nucleus is mainly water and gases, all frozen and mixed together with bits of rock and metal.

As a comet orbits closer to the Sun, the ice begins to change from a solid into a gas. The gas carries away some of the dust particles and spreads out around the nucleus in a large cloud called a coma. Sunlight causes the particles in the coma to glow. The coma of an average comet is sixty thousand miles across but contains only a little material spread out very thin.

This is a photo of the bright coma of Comet Giacobini-Zinner. The image was specially processed through a computer to show levels of brightness. The comet's motion causes background stars to show as streaks.

As a comet approaches the Sun, the pressure of radiation from the Sun and the solar wind (a stream of charged particles) sweeps the gases of the coma away from the Sun. The glowing gases form a straight tail that can grow to as much as ninety million miles long, but in many fainter comets no tail is ever seen.

A second tail of dust particles sometimes appears. The dust tail is slightly curved and usually shorter than the gas tail. In this computer-colored photo of Comet West, each color represents a different level of brightness. The broad, fan-shaped part of the tail is dust; the straight, narrow tail is gas.

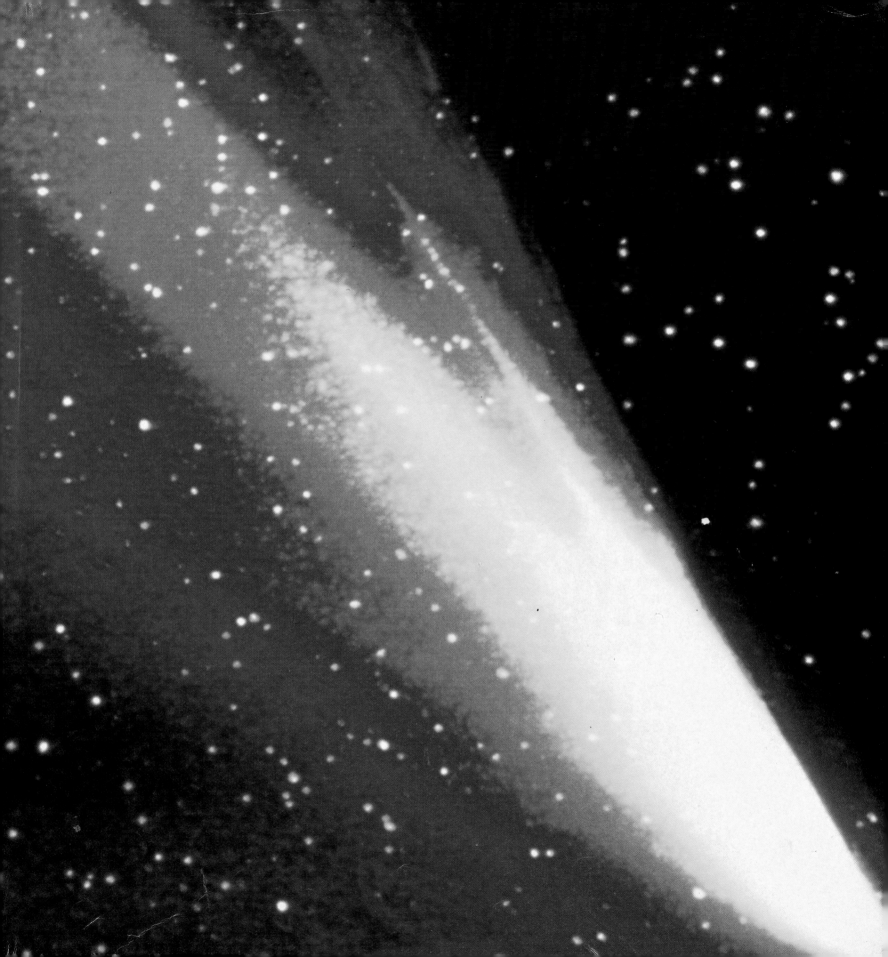

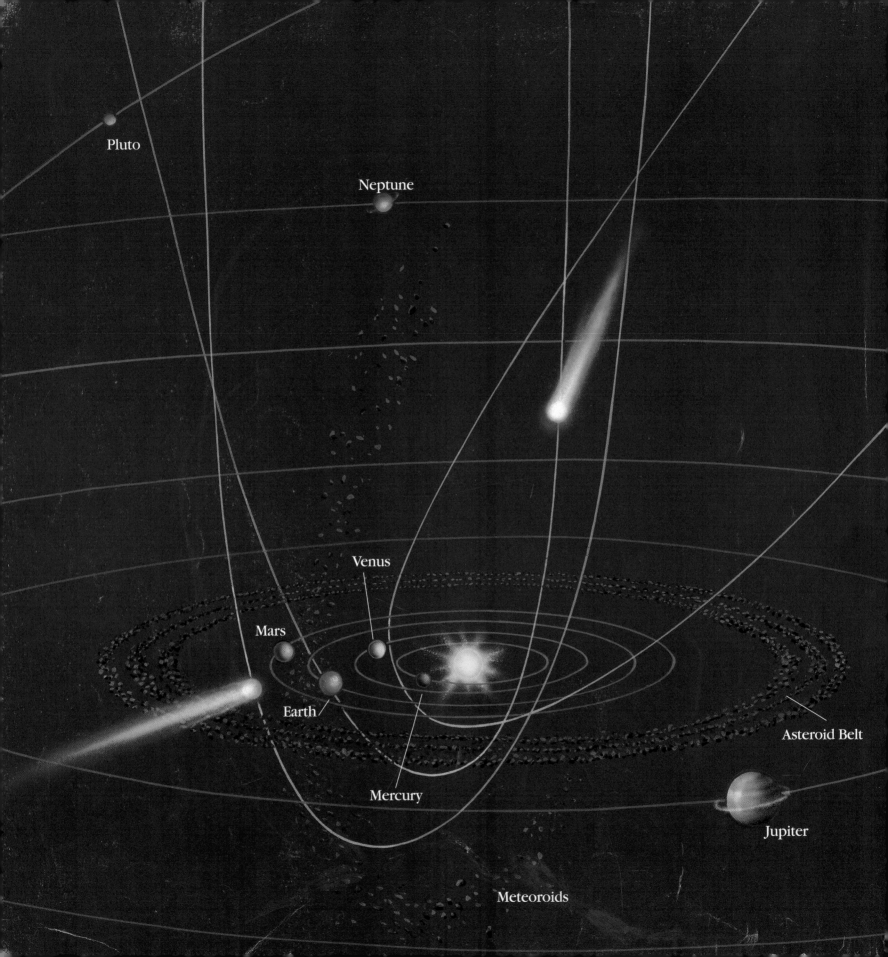

Most comet orbits are oval-shaped—long and stretched out rather than round. This drawing shows what happens to the tail as a comet travels around the Sun. When a comet moves away from the Sun, its tail actually moves *in front* of it.

Comets that take less than two hundred years to travel around the Sun are called short-period comets. Halley's comet is a short-period comet—it returns every seventy-six years. Scientists think it comes from a ring of comets that lies beyond the orbit of Pluto. This ring is named the Kuiper Belt after astronomer Gerard Kuiper, who first proposed the idea.

Many short-period comets that return in less than sixty years have orbits that go out only as far as Jupiter. The comet with the shortest known period is Encke's comet, which returns every 3.3 years.

Saturn

Uranus

How bright a comet appears depends upon its distance from the Sun and from observers on Earth. Most comets get brighter when they get close to the Sun. Some become bright very quickly, the result of a sudden increase in solar activity such as giant storms on the Sun. A few comets fade away when they approach the Sun, probably because their nucleus breaks apart.

This is Comet IRAS-Araki-Alcock 1983d. A newly discovered comet is named by the calendar year and a letter showing its order in comet sightings that year. For example, 1983d was the fourth comet sighted in 1983. Usually the comet is also named for its discoverers. Comet IRAS-Araki-Alcock was named for the Infrared Astronomy Satellite (IRAS) and the two amateur astronomers who first found the comet. This comet came closer to Earth, 2.9 million miles, than any other known comet in the past two hundred years.

The globe in the center represents our Solar System as far as the orbit of Pluto.

Most scientists think that comets are the ancient remains of the ice and dust that produced the outer planets Uranus, Neptune, and Pluto. In 1950 Jan Oort, a Dutch astronomer, suggested that a huge cloud of more than 100 billion comets surrounds the Solar System like a bubble. Comets in this Oort cloud, as it is called, are at the outer edge of the Solar System. They are hundreds of times farther away from the Sun than the most distant planets. If Pluto's orbit were the size of a quarter, the Oort cloud would be a giant beach ball fifty feet wide.

Sometimes a few comets are pushed out of their Oort cloud orbits by the gravitational force of a nearby star. Some of these long-period comets begin to follow new, stretched-out orbits that loop close to the Sun and then return to the Oort cloud in journeys that take hundreds or thousands of years. Other comets are hurled into outer space and never return to the Sun.

You are far more likely to see a meteor than a comet. Bright comets are visible in the sky only once or twice in a century and stay for many days or weeks. Meteors flash in the sky every night. They happen every day, too, but we usually can't see them in the Sun's glare.

Meteor flashes are also called falling or shooting stars. But meteors are not stars. Stars are suns far beyond our Solar System. Meteors begin as meteoroids, bits of rock or metal that orbit around the Sun. We can't see them in space because they are too small and too dark.

But sometimes meteoroids plunge into Earth's atmosphere at speeds faster than a bullet. The friction produced by rubbing against air particles makes them glow red-hot, and they are then called meteors. We see the bright flash for only a few seconds. The streak in this photo is a meteor that lasted for twelve seconds, longer than most.

Meteors come much closer to the Earth than comets. Some are brighter than the brightest star and are called fireballs. This daylight fireball appeared early one afternoon in August 1972 and was photographed over Jackson Lake in Wyoming. It burned for a hundred seconds and left a trail stretching 915 miles. Moving at more than thirty thousand miles per hour, the fireball came as close as thirty-six miles from the ground before being bounced out into space, like a thrown rock skipping across the surface of a pond.

An astronomer who saw the fireball said that its brightness was between that of the full Moon and the Sun. Had it landed, the meteorite would have been more than 250 feet across, nearly as big as a football field, and weighed over one million tons.

Several times each year you can see more than a dozen meteors in an hour in the same part of the night sky. This is called a meteor shower. It occurs when Earth passes through an old comet orbit and collides with some of the particles remaining from the comet's nucleus. Each year, Earth passes through the old comet path at about the same date. The Leonids, for example, are meteors from rocks left behind in the orbit of Comet Temple-Tuttle. When the Leonids appear in mid-November, they seem to come from the direction of the constellation (a group of stars) named Leo.

In 1966 the Leonid meteor shower was so intense that it was called a meteor storm. It was the greatest meteor storm in recorded history. At one point, meteors were falling at a rate of forty per second, equal to about 150,000 meteors per hour. This photo taken by an observer at Kitt Peak in Arizona shows dozens of Leonid meteors in the area of the Big Dipper during a forty-three-second time exposure.

Perhaps as many as 100 million meteoroids enter the Earth's atmosphere every day. Most are just tiny specks of rock and burn up in an instant. But some become dazzling fireballs and then fall to the surface. A meteor that reaches Earth's surface is called a meteorite.

Most meteorites look like ordinary rocks and are hard to find unless someone sees them fall. But meteorites that fall on Antarctica are easier to find, even after many years. Meteorites that fall in Antarctica are buried in the snow and ice. Sometimes the ice moves or the wind blows away the snow cover and the meteorites are seen by a searching helicopter.

Nine out of every ten meteorites are stony meteorites, mostly chondrites. Chondrites contain small glassy globs called chondrules, from a Greek word meaning grains. Scientists think that chondrites may have formed when the planets took shape out of the fiery cloud of dust and gas that surrounded our young Sun billions of years ago.

This stony meteorite, found in Antarctica, is not like any Earth rock, but rather very much like rocks brought back from the highlands of the Moon by the Apollo astronauts. Still another stony meteorite found in Antarctica contains glassy materials that some scientists believe may have come from Mars.

Another kind of meteorite (pictured below) is mostly iron. These iron meteorites may also contain nickel. They do not look like ordinary rocks and they stick to magnets, so they are easier to find than stony meteorites. A third group of meteorites, called stony irons, are about half stone and half nickel iron.

Asteroids are the largest of the space rocks. Most of them circle the Sun between the orbits of Mars and Jupiter in a zone called the asteroid belt. Many of the more than three thousand known asteroids are only a few miles across, and all of them together would weigh much less than the Moon. Ceres, by far the largest asteroid, is about six hundred miles across. Pallas and Vesta are next in size, at around 350 miles in diameter.

This is a photo of asteroid Gaspra taken by the *Galileo* spacecraft in 1991. Gaspra looks like a large potato in space, about twelve miles long and seven miles wide.

Some asteroids have spun out of the main belt to follow different orbits. Several dozen Trojan asteroids share the same orbit as Jupiter. The Apollo asteroids swing across Earth's orbit and approach the Sun much like some comets. In 1937 a small Apollo asteroid, Hermes, came within half a million miles of Earth. That's considered a close miss in space.

Will an asteroid or a large meteorite ever hit Earth? Many large objects have hit our planet in the past and left behind huge hollows in the ground called impact craters. The largest of these is the 4,150-foot-wide and six-hundred-foot-deep Barringer Crater near Winslow, Arizona. It was probably made by an iron meteorite slamming into the ground fifty thousand years ago.

Some scientists say that an even larger impact sixty-five million years ago resulted in the dinosaurs becoming extinct. Could a comet, large meteorite, or asteroid have caused other large extinctions of animals and plants in the past? Scientists are still not sure.

We know of hundreds of comets and thousands of asteroids, and each day Earth encounters millions of meteors. Many more will be discovered in the future. Some of these space travelers date back to the very beginning of our Solar System, 4.6 billion years ago. By learning about these rocky or icy chunks, we may discover clues that will help us solve some of the mysteries of the Solar System and of our own planet.